INFLUENCING
Generation Next

LANE ARNOLD

Copyright © 2018 Lane Arnold
All rights reserved
First Edition

PAGE PUBLISHING, INC.
New York, NY

First originally published by Page Publishing, Inc. 2018

ISBN 978-1-64350-010-2 (Paperback)
ISBN 978-1-64350-011-9 (Digital)

Printed in the United States of America

SPECIAL THANKS

I would like to give a special thanks to my spiritual parents, Pastor's Jeff and Eileen Hackleman. They believed in me at a young age and gave me opportunity to start fulfilling my dreams when I had nothing to offer but a passion for God. When I was in high school, I had the privilege of helping lead worship behind Pastor Eileen. I am so grateful for her giving me room to grow and teaching me the greatest key of all in leading people into worship—that is you must first enter into the presence of God yourself but make sure you leave the door open so everyone else can follow.

Pastor Jeff gave me my first opportunity to preach when I was eighteen years old. He placed me in situations that called out the greatness inside of me. He gave me spiritual responsibilities and physical tasks that I didn't know how to accomplish, but by God's grace, I rose to the occasion. God used those opportunities of growth to build in me the character, faith, love, and stamina that I would need to soar into my destiny.

I would like to thank them for their unwavering commitment to speak God's faith and life into the next generation. They have been a dispenser of the supernatural, uncompromising love of God for almost four decades. Thank you, Pastors for living your lives for the cause of the gospel of Jesus Christ and for your heart that you have unselfishly poured out to see generations rise up and win in life. The world will never be the same because of you.

With my wife Lisa Arnold

With my three sons from oldest to youngest
Paul, Judah and Levi

INTRODUCTION

Unlocking the Door to the Next Generation's Potential

This generation is fierce, relentless, and passionate. They love breaking rules and never sticking with the status quo. Because they have broken the molds we have set before them, we call them reckless and irresponsible. But I believe they've been created by God, exactly how they are, to bring the greatest move of God the earth has ever seen. Deep down at the center of their core, there is a compulsion to do something great, something different, something that will change their world. An urge to leave their mark, to make a difference. The sad truth is that the vast majority of them have been counted out by the generation preceding them. At a glance, we have labeled them as rebellious troublemakers and dreamers. The very ones that were supposed to applaud them, hone them, and even direct them have given up on them.

If we fail to touch the next generation, fail to grab their heart and pour the love of God into it, then it all stops with us. If we don't stop and take time to invest in them, then what are we living for? What is our purpose? My friend, I'm here to tell you that life is not a forty-yard dash, nor is it a marathon, but a relay. And as any good runner knows, the handoff is the most important part of the race. You can run swiftly, play by all the rules, and pass everyone up, but if you don't get the handoff right, you lose. Not only do you lose, but the whole team loses. The runner after you may be skilled and longing to have the baton passed to them, or they may be unprepared and afraid, but if the baton is never passed, they don't even have a chance.

You may say, "I have nothing to offer. I can't relate with this generation. I don't understand them, and they don't understand me. So how could I ever make a difference in their world?" Please understand this truth. It's not about wearing the same clothes that they wear, nor listening to the same music they listen to. It's not about learning the latest technology or talking the latest street slang. It's not about being raised on the same side of the tracks they were, nor clicking with them because you have the same personality as they do. It's not even about you going through the same abuses and hell on earth they've had to live with. Let me explain. You could relate with them in every area mentioned and still fail miserably at impacting their life for the good. Many of their peers and Media figures have proven this point. These people may dress the same as them but that doesn't mean they are truly making a difference in their eternal lives.

Making a positive difference in this next-generations destiny is based on one thing: LOVE. Yes, love. Not the four letter word that we see thrown around as if it is something you fall in and out of. No. I'm talking about God's love. First Corinthians 13 kind of love. This is a timeless unconditional love that breaks all barriers and never fails.

The young people of this world are in need of God's love so desperately, but they don't even know that is what their heart is longing for. They reach out grasping for anything that could help them fill this void, like a drowning man reaching for a lifesaver. Many turn to drugs, alcohol, sex, cutting, homosexuality, secret identities on the internet, popularity, bullying, money, metrosexual lifestyles, cars, gangs, crime, even family and friends. But none of these can fill the void in their heart. So they continue a search that many times ends up in a downward spiral.

No matter what your background, color, or style is; no matter what kind of phone you own or car you drive; no matter what school you went to—old school, new school, or the school of hard knocks—if you have the genuine love of God in your heart, then you have what this generation needs. You have in your possession the key to their happiness and fulfillment, the key to their dreams, the key to their destiny. It is time for us to use this key to unlock the door that leads to their destiny.

In this book, I will lay out ten ways to reach the next generation, enabling them to find their full potential in Christ. Each way is rooted and grounded in love. No matter if you are a parent, grandparent, pastor, politician, professional athlete, celebrity, business person, or just someone who cares, if you grab hold of this, you can truly make a difference in your world. Not only in today's world, but in every generation that is to come because you passed the baton.

Chapter 1

Compassion Will Soften the Hardest Heart (Matthew 9:36)

You've heard the saying, "People don't care how much you know until they know how much you care." Well, this is true now more than ever. Young people can see through fakeness from a mile away. A fake smile, compliment, or even fake love will never get past them because they've seen so much counterfeit acting already. They don't need more counterfeit. What they need to see is the real thing.

Compassion is not feeling sorry for somebody or having pity on them. No, it's a fire that burns inside of you, which compels you to help someone else. You know you have compassion for someone when you want the quality of their life to be better, and in helping them, there's nothing in it for you. No strings are attached. Your compassion for them is unconditional. This compassion is always 100 percent of the time, proven out by acts of love. Jesus is the greatest example of this kind of love. Jesus was moved with compassion to heal the sick. When the blind man saw, and the paralytic walked, no one could convince them that Jesus did not love them. Their lives were forever changed.

In our lives, simple acts of compassion to help young people speaks to them right where they are. This can be as simple as a genuine friendly smile or as big as paying for their college tuition. My wife and I were youth pastors at Family Faith Church for twenty-two years. In those years, we have seen, countless times, the toughest individuals be completely won over by just a few acts of kindness. They were not just looking for a place to hang out and have fun, but for a place of acceptance and love. They were in search of someone who would step up in life and fight for them. They wanted someone who would love them enough to actually discipline them. It takes love and compassion to discipline someone. As a parent disciplines their child, they are showing they have compassion by walking out their love for them. Young people may not totally understand this concept up front, but they can sense the compassion from someone who loves them enough to tell them they need to change. Now if you try doing this with the wrong heart or for the wrong reason, you will completely lose them—sometimes forever. For example, if you are just sick and tired of putting up with their disrespect and you react harshly and without wisdom, then you may have lost them before the first word is said. They can instinctively tell if you are correcting them out of love or sheer aggravation.

God-given compassion will also compel you to get involved with their life. I know we are all busy and have so much going on in our lives, especially in today's culture, but again I ask this question, "What are we living for?" God or ourselves? Time is a very precious commodity. Everything else in life can be replenished, but not time. We have what amount of time we've been given and that's it. When young people see us spending our time on them, it gives them a sense of worth. Even if they tell us that they do not want to spend time with us, they can still see when we value them. It might not happen at first, but eventually we will win them over.

Different times I have bought a teenager food or taken them with me to work out. I could tell immediately the change in their countenance when I asked them to come be a part of my life. But more importantly, and in many cases, the only way to get your foot in the door of their hearts is to go on their turf and get involved in their life. There are many ways to get involved in their lives. Maybe you can go to their sports game, attend their graduation, actually go to their house, visit them when they're sick, sit in their room and talk, "try" to play video games with them, or send messages by text and Facebook. The list goes on and on. Don't think that these things are just activities or time consumers in your day. The importance of spending this time connecting with them is immeasurable. This time creates a door to their souls. When you enter through this door, you may say exactly the same things you said before, but because the person's perspective of you has changed they will receive what you have to say. What I'm saying is that true compassion will grant you access.

Then they hear you and see you in a completely different light. They actually want to hear what you have to say. Your words and opinions take on weight and meaning to them, not because you told them something to do, but because you showed them you cared. You proved to them that they have worth in your eyes. Again, you don't have to be good at what they're good at, and you don't have to know all the latest technology or understand everything that they do. Just be there.

For a young person, just knowing that somebody cares enough to show up to their game brings confidence and courage to them. It brings out the best in them, and it also brings out the best in their relationship with you. Knowing that someone cares gives them strength to fight off thoughts of depression and loneliness. It gives them confidence to be the best that they can be. All this stems from you just caring enough to show up in their lives.

Of course, you can cancel out all the good that you've done by tearing them down with a ton of negative criticism. Make sure no ulterior motives and emotions ever dictate what is said. This will have the exact opposite effect of what's been discussed in this chapter. You need to give positive feedback that's heartfelt and true. If you give compliments that are blatantly untrue and unrealistic, then they will look at this as sarcasm or hot air, and you will lose any positive influence in the relationship you have gained.

These acts of kindness, when fueled by compassion, completely change your relationship with a young person. It earns you a place in their heart. Now, in their eyes you have the right to correct them, the right to show them things, and the right to receive their love. If there is a young person that I've just met, and I see them doing something wrong, I am very careful about correcting them. If I have not earned their respect, then chances are as soon as I step into the situation, their attitude will be, "And who are you?" If at all possible, I try to get to know them a little, show them I care, and then gently work on molding them. These acts of compassion soften the clay. If you try to bend and mold hard clay, it just breaks; but if you pour into it the water of love, it becomes pliable.

This generation needs love more than anything else. Mother Teresa put it this way, "We can cure disease with medicine but the only cure for loneliness, despair, and hopelessness is love. There are many in the world who are dying for a piece of bread, but there are many more dying for a little love." This is so true with today's youth. God's love in us is the answer to all of their questions, problems, and heartaches. It's also the key to their God-given destiny.

Chapter 2

Passion: The Ultimate Magnet

Passion is an eye-opener for this generation. It is a hidden force that pulls in the masses. Everything has shifted to the extreme. Ordinary-contemporary has now become unacceptable. Now we have extreme skiing, extreme sky diving, extreme free running, extreme fighting, extreme TV. The list goes on and on. Why, all of a sudden, does everything have to be extreme in order to be accepted and get good ratings? It's because the word *extreme* denotes passion, and this generation was made for passion. They have it in their DNA.

God has a great plan and purpose for this generation. They have been saved until now like a diamond hidden in a cave. Like a secret weapon brought out to end a war. God has said that the latter rain will be greater than the former. Because there is greatness ingrained in them, they naturally gravitate toward passion. They are looking for a cause to live for, to stand for, even to die for!

Many times I've seen teens run as far and as fast as they can from church because they see Christians who are ashamed to admit that they believe in Jesus. There is nothing more repulsive to this generation than someone who is ashamed of who they are. But anyone, no matter what they stand for, who is unashamed and passionate about what they do, will capture the attention and eventually the loyalty of this generation as a whole. There are recording artists, movie stars, and sports figures who are unashamedly passionate about their skills and lifestyle. I may not agree with all of their views on God, morals, or love, but we all should pay attention to the driving passion in their lives that has led them not only to success, but, more importantly, to have great influence with young people. It is because of this drive that many of our sons and daughters have their posters hanging in their room.

We, as Christians, have the passion of Christ beating in our hearts. This force started by faith and fueled by love is what has helped us fulfill our destiny and is leading us now to greater things. We must let this passion in us be evident to the youth following after us. Don't be afraid to share your passions with them, even at the expense of being hurt. We must live out loud in front of them. Yes, their passions are different than ours and probably totally foreign to anything we've done, but it's passion that connects two hearts, not the activity.

We must not only be passionate about what we have done, but even more importantly, we must remain passionate and positive about the future, ours, and theirs. There is nothing that will crush their dreams faster than a mentor being completely pessimistic about the future. We must show them a gleam of hope, a light at the end of the tunnel. We are commissioned by God to passionately give this generation a hope for tomorrow.

I know we live in a very volatile world. There are dangers of war, failing governments, and ever increasing natural disaster all around us. And yes, this young generation needs to be educated and prepared but never throw in the towel on them. Don't become so negative about everything around them that they lose all hope for their future. We must strive to do greater things and encourage them to do the same because we know, as believers in Christ, our best days are always ahead of us. In this world, you can rest assured that they are getting doom and gloom predictions everywhere they turn. We need to bring them the gospel, which literally means "good news." When we are more passionate and happy about the Gospel than anything else they see, their heads will start to turn.

A passion for tomorrow is always more exciting and attractive than people who have what I call the "good ole days" syndrome. Now don't get me wrong, the story of your past could be the very thing someone needs to hear in order to be what God has called them to be but never put more emphasis on your past than you do on your future. Your testimony could be the nudge someone needs that gives them confidence to do God's best for them and not settle for anything less. Never downplay your past, just don't get stuck in it. Let's celebrate the past and learn from it without thinking that the best days are behind us. The story of your past may hold the key to unlock chains of suicide and alcoholism or to start successful business and ministries.

When we celebrate the past, enjoy the present, and look forward to the future, we become the wind under a youth's wings. They will want what you are having even if they have no idea what it is. This is called shining your light. Your passion for Christ, which gives you a hope for tomorrow, will be a light in their dark places. As a matter of fact, the darker the place, the brighter a light shines. The worse the world gets, the more influence we will have by simply having faith and living for God with all our heart.

Chapter 3

Listening, the Pathway to Influence

Listening is one of the single most important keys when it comes to gaining access to influence in anyone's life, but particularly in the life of young people. I'm not just talking about hearing what someone has to say, but truly listening to them. True listening is when you pay attention to where they are coming from. You look for past experiences, abuses, and relationships that have brought them to where they are at that moment. Not only do you hear what they say, but you see what they mean. When someone begins to listen in this manner, it literally unlocks the door to the soul so that the one talking can share things that had been long forgotten but not let go of.

But how do you listen if no one wants to talk? In order for you to be a good listener, you must first get someone to open up to you. Have you ever known someone who only wanted to talk about themselves? Did you feel that they cared about you and wanted to hear what you had to say? Probably not. When someone is focused on themselves, their agenda and their feelings get in the way of them hearing what anyone else has to say. This makes for a poor listener. You cannot be focused on your own agenda and your own feelings while truly listening and understanding someone else. You must want to understand, not just be understood.

Here's the key: the best listeners always ask the best questions. When you start asking the right questions, you open the door of someone's heart. It shows them that you really do want to hear their side, their pain, their story.

Wayne Northup, a pastor friend of mine, who is also an evangelist has traveled around the United States talking to hundreds of thousands of students. At the end of every assembly he has ever done, he asks the students, "What's your story?" He asks them this because he knows they are longing to be heard. Many times I have seen shifts is my relationship with someone just because I listened to their viewpoints, hurts, or concerns. They don't necessarily want or even need answers to their problems up front. They just need to be given the surety that someone cares enough to listen. Then, after a foundation of trust has been established, they will be open to answers.

When you ask someone about their life, you give them a voice. One of the top needs of any generation, especially this one, is simply to be heard. When a segment of society is ignored or labeled as "too ignorant to listen to," you can rest assured that bitterness, anger, and violence will follow. Dr. Martin Luther King once said, "Violence is the language of the unheard." This generation desperately wants to be heard.

Remember you, as a loving mentor, have what this generation needs to survive and to thrive; but in order to impart it, you must give them a voice by lending your ear. And more than that, you must feel their pain. Just because you listen to someone does not mean that you condone everything they have done, but it means you have heard them and love them anyway. In spite of their past . . . when they know you love them no matter what, they will begin to open up their ears and hearts to what you have to say as you pour God's love back inside of them.

Chapter 4

Morals: Old Answers to New Problems

Psalms 100:5, "For the LORD is good; his mercy is everlasting; and his truth endureth to all generations."

If there was only one thing I could say in this book, only one principle I could leave with you, it would be this one: pass down the godly moral system that is inside of you, for it is the only hope that the next generation has for a happy and fulfilling life. Nothing can take the place of having morals, and nothing can bring the stability it grows in one's life. Many people have diluted and distorted what it means to have morals. Today's society claims that truth is relative, and that as long as you follow what you think is right, you are a good moral person. The problem with that concept is this: just because you believe something is true does not make it true. No more than believing that something is right makes it right. But God our Father has put a moral compass in us that always leads us back to his Word. The true meaning of having morals simply means that you know the biblical difference between right and wrong and want to do right because it pleases God.

The Ten Commandments are the foundation of biblical morals and were given by God to protect his children from the hardships that come from living an immoral lifestyle. They are the greatest set of laws ever written. These laws were endorsed and quoted by Jesus himself! Passing on this foundation for success should be a top priority for every generation.

There is an epidemic that has swept across the face of the earth in the last fifty years. It is a movement away from simple God-given right and wrong principles. Because of this, many young people have lost their hope for true happiness. This lack of godly direction has completely destroyed entire nations. On the surface, it may look like foreign affairs or economical climates are what make societies rise and fall, but the root cause always traces back to the lack of morals. The absence of godly morals is like the HIV virus; it slowly deteriorates the immune system, crippling the body's only defense mechanism. A person with AIDS is not killed by the disease itself, but by some other form of sickness. It could be something as small as the common cold that actually triggers the death, but AIDS is what weakened the body to the point of being completely defenseless. This is the exact same thing that happens to a society that turns from foundational moral values. After inner strength and virtue is gone, there is no integrity to uphold the structure of a society. Without morals, there is no hope for a better tomorrow.

Now let's flip it around and look at the reverse side. If we, as Christians, pass down the godly principles that have been ingrained in us, we will bring stability and strength to the world of tomorrow—the world in which our children and grandchildren will live. This belief system, as outlined in the Bible, will guide the next generation through victories and be a lighthouse that steers them away from certain destruction.

There are some great, undeniable benefits that morals bring into a culture. First, living with godly morals gives someone the privilege of having a clean conscience, giving them courage to fight for greatness. Have you ever noticed that when you know you've done your best and treated people with honor and respect, it gives you a strength to face tomorrow with a smile? It makes you feel lighter, like you could soar through any obstacle that came your way. But when you have done someone wrong, and you know it was wrong, this hidden strength leaves, making it hard to do even the simplest of things. The only way to have true fulfillment is to have a clean, guilt-free conscience. You could be the richest person in the world, but if you don't have a pure conscience, it's all for nothing because guilt and shame will eat away at your heart until there is nothing left but bitterness and sorrow. But doing what's right, even after you've done something wrong, makes the heaviest heart heal.

The second benefit to living with morals is that it brings you honor. People may not like you or want you to succeed for whatever reason, but as you treat others honestly and love everyone God's way, you will inevitably be honored—not only for what you've done, but for what you have become. A person who is trustworthy and loyal always gains the respect of others, even their enemies.

Having morals also brings joy. A moral system builds an atmosphere in which joy can thrive. In order for someone to have an ongoing flow of joy, there must be stability that comes from a right standing with God or being righteous. This doesn't mean that a person has to be perfect. The Bible says no one except Jesus has ever been perfect, and if someone claims to be, they are a liar. No, a righteous person is just someone with a pure heart doing their best to please God. So righteousness brings stability, which in turn makes way for joy. I'm not talking about the feeling of happiness, though that is great to have and will come often, but rather an ongoing overtone of joy that can be brought into every situation. This joy comes from the heart and is not something that is fleeting. Joy is what brings the flavor to life. It makes it fun and exciting. The young people of this world are longing to have it, but without moral guidance, sporadic happiness is all they will ever know.

The greatest benefit having morals brings to a generation is that they produce healthy families that are bonded together by love. This one thing is the element in which the success of a nation hinges. When a family lives by biblical values, the children in that household are actually groomed for success. When there is mutual love between the mom and dad, the children get to enjoy childhood. They feel protected, secure, and strengthened by just seeing their parents remain faithful to each other.

Now I've seen many people who were raised in horrible situations turn into champions in life. These people adopted morals without having a family unit. The thing is, 100 percent of them had someone who came into their life and mentored or influenced them in some way. But as I talked to them throughout my life, they all shared the same desire to be a part of a loving family.

The residual benefits of passing down morals are endless. You could never truly measure the worth or effects of morals in a society, but you can certainly see the greatness it brings out of people.

The last thing I must share about morals is that they are caught, not taught. We must be prepared to say, "Do as I do; not just as I say." The fact is that a child or someone looking up to us cannot hear what we are saying over the sound of our actions. So we should live these morals out in front of them as we teach them. Of course we will fail, sometimes miserably. But if we repent and humbly learn from our mistakes in front of the people we are leading instead of covering everything up they will learn one of the greatest lessons of all; How to get back up. When a leader covers their faults, pretending to be Superman the next generation will either be tempted to give up because they know they could never attain this perfection, or live in denial which will drastically stunt their emotional and spiritual growth. Living out Godly morals through love, repentance and transparency will give us credibility and honor in the eyes of this generation. The words of someone who lives out what they believe have weight and influence. These words are tried and true, not just theory.

Chapter 5

Faithfulness, the Deciding Factor

Faithfulness and stability are two of the most unsung heroes of our day. They are not glamorous or outspoken, but when all else fails, they will prove themselves effective. These two virtues are the weight that will tip the scales when trying to bring positive change in a young person's life.

There was a young man in our youth group who was miraculously saved and turned wholeheartedly from a lifestyle of gang violence and crime to Jesus. Every week, he would bring more of his friends and family members to church, and every week, they would get saved. I started inviting him into my life, to come with me and do whatever I did. I didn't understand anything about his background nor did he understand mine, but over time, we grew closer and closer.

One day, I picked him up from his house, like I had done so many times before; but this day was different. As we rode together, his countenance started to change, and tears began streaming down his face. This was very out of character for him. I had never seen him cry before, and I've never seen him do it since. Then he said something that would change my life forever. He looked me straight in the eye and said, "You are the only person who has ever been there for me no matter what.

Thank you for never giving up on me. You'll never know the difference you've made in my life." It was like time stood still. I was so humbled, yet so blessed all at the same time.

Until then, I thought I was limited, by some unspoken rule, to whose life I could touch according to what I had gone through in my life. But it was that day that I realized you didn't have to be an ex-gang member to reach gangs, and you didn't have to be an ex-addict to reach drug addicts, you only had to love someone with the love of Christ faithfully. This and this alone was enough. Being a rock that doesn't blow around with the wind or change with emotional hype is priceless, and this is longed for in the world we live. You can never measure its value. Why do parents have so much influence in their children's lives? Because they are constantly there. Why do parents who are not there have such a profoundly negative effect on their children? Because they are constantly *not* there. And why do good, positive coaches have such a knack for pulling the best out of their players? Because they are there day in and day out to train them, not allowing them to settle for average.

The older generation has this faithfulness in them. They learned to grit their teeth, stand strong against the wind, pull themselves up buy their bootstraps, and hold fast to the Lord's hand no matter what. This was ingrained into them through mentors and life. These veterans of life have a staying power that youth desperately need in order to reach their full potential. It is up to us as the preceding generation to be there for them, showing ourselves constant and worthy of imitation. I've heard many people disagree with this concept saying, "No, Lane, we want them to be followers of Christ, not followers of us." This is only partly true. Here's how the Apostle Paul put it when talking to the next generation of his day. "Follow me as I follow Christ." We may be the only Jesus this generation will ever see. We can't expect them to put their faith in God, which they can't see, before they actually see Him in us who they can see. The loving faithfulness and stability in our day-to-day lives will be the instruments that open their eyes to see the good in us they so desperately need.

The 2015 Roar Rally:
600 teens gave their lives to Christ that night.

SEALS Bootcamp Leadership Retreat.
(Saints Evangelizing all Lost Souls)

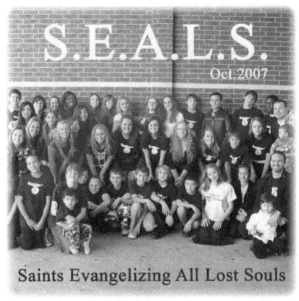

SEALS Leadership graduating class of 2007.

Lane inspiring the next generation during the Friday Night Live youth service they had for over 22 years.

10 to 30 teens gave their lives to Christ almost every Friday for over two decades in the Family Faith Church Gym, also known as the Harvest Center.

Lisa teaching this Generation how to draw close to God.

Chapter 6

A Father to the Fatherless

First Corinthians 4:15 says, "For though ye have ten thousand instructors in Christ, yet have ye not many fathers: for in Christ Jesus I have begotten you through the gospel."

Today's young generation is so desperately in need of fathers. I'm not just talking about someone who passes on their last name or someone who only tells them what to do or what not to do, but rather someone that tells them, "You are mine and I am yours." Someone to prefer them and to love them as their own. There is no counterfeit that will work in its place and no hype that will compare to this love. It has no bounds and can bring someone back up from the lowest of depths.

Throughout this book, I have discussed many different types of discipleship. Each are essential steps on the way to raising a generation of champions, but this is the pinnacle of mentoring. Fathering someone is the highest form of discipleship, and when done from the heart and for the right reasons, it is extremely dear to God's heart. So much so that God is known as, and refers to himself as, "Father." This is because it most accurately depicts the kind of love he has for us.

Now if you are a female, I don't want you to think this chapter is excluding you because of your gender. When I say fathering, you can liken it to parenting. It simply means you care for someone in the next generation as your own and are willing to stand beside them, just because you love them, with no strings attached. This is the God kind of love, and that is why it is so powerful.

But the problem is that you can't father everyone. I truly believe we can evangelize the world through massive concerts, have crusades that reach the nations, even utilize television to strengthen the church body (numbering into the hundreds of millions that view), but we can only father the few God has brought close into our lives. When I say God will bring them, I don't mean he will make them come beat on our door. We still must go and reach people with the love of God, but of the people we touch, the Lord will choose the ones we are to "bring under our wing." Jesus reached and sincerely cared for the crowds here on earth, but he only discipled twelve. Out of the twelve disciples, I believe he only fathered three: Peter, James, and John. But with these three, he started a movement that changed the world!

Not everyone is ready to be discipled, even fewer are ready to be fathered, and still even less are ready to be fathered by you. Sometimes you may have the right person, but they simply are not ready. If they are pushed into something prematurely, they will wind up resenting you or they will run the opposite direction as fast as they can. It is imperative that we let them be drawn to us by love as we continually stand faithful in their lives.

When you have someone in your life who has been influenced by God's love in you, you can start helping him or her find God's path by teaching them simple Bible truths. You will soon be able to discern who is ready and who is pulling away and shutting you out. That doesn't mean the ones that are ready will wholeheartedly accept everything you say. (Only people who are trying to flatter you to get something do this.) It means that even through disagreement, there is still a strong underlying respect that is evident after the smoke clears.

When you start to discipline (disciple) someone out of love and a pure heart, as stated earlier in this book, they will feel a genuine concern and care from you. As God, the father, disciplines his children, he is distinguishing them as his own. For example, if there were twenty neighborhood kids outside in the street playing ball, and it was supper time, you would call out to your own saying, "Come on. Let's eat." And if they didn't pay attention, you would make them come in with the parental tone that gets the job done. If a stranger was observing, they would automatically assume the specific ones you addressed were yours. I'm definitely not saying that God will punish us by pain or make us suffer. This is a misconception that many people have of God. He doesn't put diseases on people so they can learn humility, and he doesn't give his child a "scorpion when they ask for an egg" (Luke 11:12). But he does lead, correct, and bring "godly sorrow to" those he loves so they can grow. We should in turn do the same for those he has placed under our care.

But how do you know who is the right one to father or who is ready, and what do you do when you find them? Go back to Jesus, our ultimate example. When he first came to Peter, he said, "Let's go fishing." Peter's first words were full of excuses explaining why he couldn't do what Jesus had asked of him. Then he said, very hesitantly, "But if you say so, I will go." Even after he obeyed and the most famous fishing trip of all times happened in his boat, he got hung up on his own insecurities by saying, "Please leave me alone. I'm not worthy." Then Jesus, still believing in Peter, made one more request. He said, "Come follow me, and I will make you a fisher of men." What if Jesus would have given up after the first wave of unbelief, or the first line of sarcasm? One of the chief disciples would never have been raised up to become the great apostle, Peter.

Let's look at another situation that happened to Jesus. The rich young ruler met the Savior on a road and asked how to get to heaven. That was a pretty legit question. After telling him to obey the Bible, Jesus asked him to sell all his belongings, give offerings to the poor, and follow Him. This wealthy young man was literally being called by God right then and there. But he chose with his own will not to answer the call. Once the rich young ruler turned and walked away, Jesus kept on going, and the young man chose to follow his own path.

Sometimes everything may be right: you, the timing, and the person, but they must choose to follow. That's not to say he wouldn't have another chance, but Jesus went about his business and let the man choose for himself. If this happened to Jesus, don't feel bad if it ever happens to you. Just keep on loving and leading.

When you feel that a certain person truly sees that you love them and keeps an underlying respect for you even when they get close to you, it's time to seek God for wisdom about "taking them in." In order to do this, you must prefer them as your own. There are so many youth whose hearts are breaking for someone to prefer them, not because they are better than the rest, and not because they have proven themselves, but because they are a spiritual son or daughter to you.

If you are a parent, think about how you watch a race, ball game, or award ceremony when your child is involved. It doesn't matter who else shows up, you are automatically biased toward your own child. When you prefer your child, they know that you believe in them. This brings security that will stick with them throughout their whole lives. Security leads to confidence, confidence leads to strength, and strength gives them the ability to make good decisions uninhibited by insecurities that stem from what they "never had." Your total unrestrained love is like medicine that strengthens their immune system enabling them to bounce back and overcome adversity.

One thing I love doing is going to minister to inmates in prison. There are thousands of great people who are behind bars who just need to be loved and given a second chance. Throughout the years, I have heard hundreds of different stories, but not once have I ever heard an inmate tell me they had a loving father in their life—one who was always there for them and believed in them. The fact is, it wasn't the juvenile or inmate who was delinquent, but the parent. Having someone who constantly shows they have faith in you strengthens your self-image. This factor is irreplaceable. The way someone views them-self today will become reality tomorrow unless someone intervenes and changes that perception. This is where a father figure can make such a difference.

Security and protection combined create another facet of fathering. One of the foundational meanings of a father is one who protects. At the center of God's heart is a desire to shelter those who cannot protect themselves, and he promises many times throughout his Word to reward those who follow Him in doing this. When there is a loving parental figure in someone's life, it brings an unseen umbrella of protection. This covering helps bring safety as they are nourished, while teaching them how to make successful decisions. Then someone can stand on their own two feet in the midst of life's challenges.

Remember the biblical story of the foolish man building his house on the sand and the wise man building his on the Rock. When the storms of life came, one had a foundation to uphold him, but the other had nothing to stand on. I don't think the foolish man wanted everything he had worked for to be destroyed by the storms of life. I don't even think that he had anything against building a house on the Rock. The reason he built his house on the sand was because it was all he knew how to do. Someone may argue that he didn't build on the rock because he was too lazy. That may be true, but laziness was what he was taught and therefore what he knew. If someone is never taught, how will they learn? We must strive to show people the way. Romans 10:14 says, "How then shall they call on him in whom they have not believed? And how shall they believe in him of whom they have not heard? And how shall they hear without a preacher?"

In nature, we know that a baby needs a mother's care to survive. Wouldn't it be ridiculous to expect an infant to make it on their own saying, "Well, if they were really healthy, they would be able to fend for themselves." Just think how repulsive the thought of someone leaving a newborn infant or even a child on the curb is. Anyone in their right mind would say that is horrible, but somehow many people don't see this in spiritual matters. They think, "Well, if this young person had a good heart, they would have been able to withstand the temptations that made them fall. Or if they really cared about others, then they wouldn't lash out in anger the way they do." Maybe they are just infants needing someone to pick them up off the curb where they were left and start to nourish them with the milk of God's common sense.

Other times, children or infants don't need to be taught anything, they simply need someone to stand up for them. In life, our children don't need to always learn from storms. Many times, they simply need to be protected from them. The time will come for them to be trained to stand up and take on any storm of life, but at first, they must just be taught how to stand. I see youth all the time who are trying to weather storms that they shouldn't even be dealing with at that point in life. They don't need someone to teach them how to get a job and support themselves at eight. No, they need someone to take them in and protect them so they can survive.

Another essential part of "fathering" is the law of needing. Everyone has a deep-rooted desire in their innermost soul to be needed. This is a God-given desire that is the glue of a family. Of course, love is the foundation of every family unit, but this desire to be needed is like gravity that holds people's feet to the ground. When someone, young or old, feels like they are not needed by anyone, a door of hopelessness opens. Once opened, despair, anxiety, resentment, and rejection soon enter, even though they were never invited. But when you are needed, this fundamental satisfaction makes sure that door is sealed tightly shut. When you need someone, just like love, you desire for them to need you back. When mixed with love, this forms a bond that strengthens the heart, causing courage to rise up in someone enabling them to fulfill their destiny. The drawback to needing and being needed is that it leaves you vulnerable to that person, but never forget this principle: without vulnerability, there is no real love.

The process of bringing someone into your life and letting them get close to your heart is not easy because it brings awkwardness to both people, especially at first. As you show them love, you become vulnerable to them, and then as they receive it and reciprocate it back, they become vulnerable to you. This vulnerability is the biggest reason why most people never take the time to become a father to the fatherless or try to let someone be a father to them. It is inconvenient and sometimes hurts. When you let your heart grow soft toward someone because you love them, automatically and involuntarily, you let your guard down toward them. This is many people's greatest fear. Yes, love can hurt; and yes, sometimes young people will not honor you the way they should, but in the words of Mother Teresa, "Do it anyway." The joy that comes from helping someone overcome life's deadly blows and still come out on top in this world is immeasurable.

Unfortunately, many of today's young generation have been hurt by everyone who has ever been close to them. This has created a breeding ground for mistrust and, in many cases, hatred; but the longing for an authority figure to show them unconditional love will outweigh the urge to pull away. When they encounter a genuine heart, God's Spirit will soften theirs, creating an opportunity for his love to be poured into them.

Being a father to the fatherless is so important to God that he said it is a foundational part of your faith. James 1:27 says, "Pure religion and undefiled before God and the Father is this, to visit the fatherless and widows in their affliction, and to keep himself unspotted from the world." God loves defending those who have no other defense. Our Father is telling us through his Word to stand up and fight for those who cannot or have not been taught how to fight for themselves. He is calling us to be a father to the fatherless in order to change their lives.

Chapter 7

Give Breath to Their Dreams

As a child, I grew up with self-esteem issues and fears of failure. I remember looking in the mirror and hating the way I looked because I was a little overweight. At a very young age, I would sit in my room and worry about never getting married or never getting a job because I wasn't good enough. I was very shy and would look down at my feet everywhere I went for fear of making eye contact with anyone. But as I grew, I remembered certain things that people in my life said and did that made me believe in myself. These moments of encouragement changed the course of my destiny.

At the age of eleven, I started to play the guitar and sing. Now I know my voice was cracking, and I probably sounded like a hot mess, but my father always took time to come and listen to me. After mowing the yard on a Saturday morning, we would sit on the porch then he would ask me to play and sing for him. He always sat there and listened to me as if I were the main event at Madison Square Garden, applauding at the end of every song. Every time without fail, he would smile and say, "Thank you for playing for me. I love to hear you sing." Those words built such confidence in me that I started leading worship at the age of twelve. Everyone wasn't singing my praises, at the time, but the right people were.

I remember my freshmen year in high school when my head football coach said, "Arnold" (I don't know why they always call you by your last name?), but anyway, he said, "You're a strong player with good heart. One day you are going to be a great athlete. Those words stuck with me and helped give me the drive to excel in sports. These were very simple things that people said to and did for me, but the effect on my life was huge.

You see, words are like construction crews. They can either build you up one brick at a time, or tear you down with a wrecking ball to ground zero. In order for someone to have protection from negative words, they must strengthen their self-image. This healthy self-perspective must be cultivated and nurtured like a tree. When the tree is young, the smallest drought or storm can destroy it. That's why it must be watered and cared for. After it grows, it "takes root." You don't have to water a fifty-foot oak tree in the middle of a dry spell because its roots have grown deep, bringing structure and stability.

Now think back to those key times in life when someone you looked up to encouraged you. Remember the feeling of strength and confidence it brought to you. Can you see the difference it made? What if they never took the time or energy out of their lives to stop what they were doing and believe in you? When we speak heartfelt positive words to people, it breathes life into their dreams. It gives them the courage to believe that not only can life be great, but that they can be great and do great things.

Just as someone's destiny can be brought to life with words of affirmation, their dreams can be shattered or, even worse, aborted before they ever draw the first breath through condescending negativity. When a young person is constantly told how bad they are, it creates a stronghold of hopelessness in their life through which everything is filtered. This is why many teenagers don't receive compliments with open arms right up front. When their dreams have been trampled on for so long, it taints everything they hear and see. A shield or front of an "I don't care" attitude is raised because they don't want those words of negativity that have killed their dreams to hurt their heart anymore. It is an act of self-preservation. But so many times, the authorities in their life label it as rebellion, starting a relentless snowball of insecurity and fear. Once this ball of broken dreams reaches the bottom of the hill, it can turn into full-grown hatred and resentment. Still, anything can be turned around through the miracle of God's love in us, but it isn't easy.

Worse than speaking negativity into someone's present is speaking death into their future, their dreams, and their surrounding world. If someone has no future accomplishments to look forward to in life, they feel broken and their self-worth is low. Life is so much more enjoyable when you know there is light at the end of the tunnel. This hope for the future will enhance the quality of their present. The sad thing is, when authority figures constantly talk about how bad the world is, how they are glad they won't be around to see the downfall of our culture, and how they feel sorry for the young people who will have to live through it, they literally fuel the negative future they speak of. Facts say there are bad things going on all around us, every day, from household violence to world-wide economic failure. Truth says, we as the Children of God, will be blessed wherever we go, and our "Descendants will be prosperous and mighty on the earth" (Psalms 112:2).

Silence is another huge dream killer. The book of Ecclesiastes says, "There is a time for silence and a time to speak." Both are important, but if we fail to speak when the youth in our lives need to hear our voice the most, we fail most miserably. If we don't speak words of encouragement, then young people in our lives will fall to the ground. Our silence gives validity to the thoughts of disgrace they are feeling. Praise may rarely be deserved, but it is an essential part of every young person's growing experience and is necessary for them to reach their full potential.

Never forget this. Our youth are the hope of tomorrow. Without them, there is no future because the future is solely what they make of it. God has given us the great honor of raising them up and blowing wind into their sails. Let us never take this for granted, for it is priceless in the eyes of God.

Chapter 8

The Theory of Relativity

In over twenty years of youth ministry, I have seen so many teens run from church because they couldn't understand the culture we had created. Our language and our methods are sometimes so foreign to them that they need a translator to tell them what is going on as soon as they step in the doors. It's like someone from the United States going to a remote tribal village in Africa that they had never heard of and trying to live there. In church, most of the time they leave not because they want to run from God, but because they don't relate with or understand anything that's going on around them. The ones who stay in church are those who are able to decipher what is being said and apply it to their life. It makes it so much easier for our young people to do this if they have someone who uses relevant methods of inspiration and teaching. The message never changes, but our methods must. This is what I call the "theory of relativity."

Now don't get me wrong. I love the whole Body of Christ, and like the Apostle Paul, I am just glad people are preaching the message of Christ. But sometimes when we hold on to the methods that were effective in reaching past generations, we lose influence on the people of today. It's almost like we are trying our best to evangelize the church when we have been commissioned to reach the world. Paul used the power of relevance throughout his whole ministry.

In 1 Corinthians 9:19–21, Paul writes to the church:

> For though I be free from all men, yet have I made myself servant unto all, that I might gain the more.
>
> And unto the Jews I became as a Jew, that I might gain the Jews; to them that are under the law, as under the law, that I might gain them that are under the law;
>
> To them that are without law, as without law (being not without law to God, but under the law to Christ), that I might gain them that are without law.
>
> To the weak became I as weak, that I might gain the weak: I am made all things to all men, that I might by all means save some.

Here he is trying to tell us that we must change our methods to reach everyone we are called to reach. In Jerusalem, he used the Law of Moses pointing to the Promised Messiah. In Athens, Greece, he used the idol image they labeled as "The Unknown God" to open their hearts to the one true Lord of all. And finally to the Romans he showed them the all-powerful king who loves his children. He used contemporary ideas from each culture to grab their attention and open their hearts to the uncompromising, unchanging Word of God.

In my early years of youth ministry, there was this one young man who loved pushing me to my limits. Later on in life, he became a stable father to his children and a personal friend to me, but it most certainly was a difficult journey. I would get so frustrated with him at times, but I could never stay mad because he would always make me laugh. I can just see God looking down in those moments and saying, "Thanks, son. I really needed some comical relief."

On this one particular night, I was preaching my heart out about "Abraham, the Father of Faith." This young man started up his usual routine of making funny gestures that mimicked me while trying to gain as big of an audience as he could, so I tried stepping it up a notch. But the more passionately I preached, the more material he had to work with. Soon, he had captivated over half the crowd, including most of my leaders. I had had enough. As the "preacher," I was going to let him have it. So I asked some of my chuckling leaders to take him to the back, telling him in my authoritative man voice, "We'll deal with this after service!" With my red flushed face, I trudged through the rest of my sermon as best I could, but I never got the crowd back that night.

As I entered the room, my mom, being one of our leaders at the time, was calmly but firmly telling him how he should act during church. She said to him in that loving tone only acquired by Mothers, "Now son, you didn't hear a word that was preached tonight did you? The young man looked up at her with eyes of certainty and said, "Of course I remember what tha man said. He was talkin' about Abraham Lincoln and stuff." All hope for the correction speech was long gone in a split second. I had to excuse myself from the room as I busted out in uncontrollable laughter. But I'll never forget the puzzled look on his face as he pointed in my direction and said, "What's so funny?"

I learned a very valuable lesson that day. It doesn't matter how "passionately" we preach or how great a Christian we have become, if we are not speaking *their* language, they will never catch *our* message. This doesn't mean that we have to change our standards nor our convictions, but rather we must adapt the way we communicate. Sometimes we must change our vocabulary, so they can grasp what we are saying. In other words, we can't go around speaking in King James language to people, especially if they have never been to church. Not only is it hard for them to understand us, but honestly, many young people are freaked out by it. We must constantly be conscious of whether or not they understand the terminology we are using. If we are not careful, the effectiveness of our message will be lost through their mistranslation.

It's not just what we say (word selection) that makes a difference, but also how we say it and in what context we use it. When a young person steps into our world, we must diagnose where they are spiritually and emotionally and what has been going on in their life to get them there. The current issue that seems to be the problem seldom is the true cause of their pain. Most times the true cause is something that happened years before and has been churning right below the surface enabling bitterness and shame to dictate their present. When we see beyond the superficial current circumstances and begin looking into their lives, we may be able to plug a Scripture or a word from God's heart into theirs. This is how people are won over.

My wife is exceptionally good at this. She can look through a hardened, rebellious front in a second and speak straight to their heart. One night during another youth service, I had to ask a group that was distracting everyone else from listening to go outside. My wife, along with several key leaders, followed them out. Then she took the ringleader aside. We knew nothing about him at the time, but later would find out that he was heavily involved in gang violence and drugs. He was high most of the time we saw him and always played out this act that nothing ever shook him. As they stood there, he started to tell Lisa how he never wanted to come back, but she abruptly interrupted him by saying, "You're called to be a preacher, aren't you?" He immediately fixed his eyes on hers and froze with the look of a child who had just been found in a game of hide-and-seek. She went on and said, "As a matter of fact, when you were a child, you told your parents you were going to be a pastor of a church, but you've been running from God for almost ten years."

Tears started to well up in his eyes as he said, "How did you know that? I've never told anyone about that."

Then she said these life-changing words: "I know you've been putting up this front so everyone will respect you, but you need to know that God loves you and still wants to use you. I want you to know that you are not alone because we love you too, and we want to see you do great things."

All he could utter was, "Yes, ma'am . . . Yes, ma'am. I . . . I know. Thank you."

My wife could have gotten frustrated and given up on him like most of the people in his life, but that's not what he needed. He needed someone to look past his facade and see the painful fears that were holding him back. She could have just said, "Oh well, I guess he doesn't want to hear our message." But instead she listened to the Holy Spirit and spoke words that showed him God's love and power all at the same time. She made the message extremely relevant to him and helped him apply it to his life. His whole demeanor changed instantly, and he was never the same.

In order to grab the hearts of this generation, we must be willing to set pride aside and break the gospel down in a way that captivates everyday people who are hurting all around us. To an infant, we bring milk in a bottle. To a mature adult, we can bring steak. Is one better than the other? Not if you balance its importance over the course of a lifetime, but to a baby, milk is not only better, it's essential for existence. Milk is the only form of nutrients it can digest. Just like we would nurture this newborn, we must speak the life of God's Word in a way people can digest. I'm certainly not saying we should water it down and let people's opinions of us dictate our message, but rather we should say what needs to be said out of a heart of love in a way that makes sense to them.

Chapter 9

The "Sound" of a Generation

If you want to see what is inside the heart and soul of a generation, just listen to the music it produces. Music is what captures the passions and ideologies of a culture. It may be heard by the natural ear, but it never stops there. Music pierces through natural senses and goes directly to one's core. The Bible describes this core in two parts: spirit and soul (1 Th. 5:23, Eph. 3:16). That's why filmmakers put music to movies. Can you imagine watching a movie with no background music? Nothing would be as touching because the door of your inner man would still be shut. Behind this door lie our most precious possessions. This is where your belief systems, lifelong passions, and love all originate. It is also where we hear God's voice of love through things like peace and conviction. Music has the power to go into this core and resonate with what is already there or challenge what has not yet been fortified.

Music can transcend social, political, generational, denominational, racial, and language barriers. It is so powerful that it can bring back emotions of an era in someone's life that had been buried and forgotten for fifty years. It can create a moment of love that melts two hearts into one, and it can bring a veteran to their knees in tears because it touched their heart with sounds of passion for their country. But God's ultimate purpose for music is worship to bring mankind close to Him.

For centuries, the church banned any new sound of music, labeling it as ungodly and sensual. The truth that they failed to see is that music is simply a carrier of lyrics. Yes, its sounds can open the heart, but when the music stops the lyrics, or message, is what remains. Instead of banning the wrong message, they banned whole genres of music, eliminating this God-given tool to reach different cultures. The church shut out rock 'n' roll to pop, soul, and funk to contemporary R and B thinking the style of music was leading people away from God.

Even certain musical instruments were looked at as sinful and thought to arouse evil desires. Fifty to one hundred years ago, the piano and violin were looked at by the church as sensual elements of the saloon and honky-tonk scene. As the church slowly adapted to each instrument, they would move this negative label to whatever was contributing to the latest sound of the day. From the piano it went to the guitar, then to the electric guitar, then to a synthesizer and so on. Some churches banned instruments all together, building entire doctrines around this concept.

When people came into the House of God, they had to listen to music that was anywhere from decades to centuries old. Many couldn't connect with the music, so they left the church. They were forced to choose between going to church and listening to styles of music that moved them.

In recent years, there has been a major shift within the church world in the area of music. For the past three decades, we have begun, not only to accept, but also to use the genres of music that have captivated our world. Anointed artists such as Petra, DC Talk, Delirious, T-Bone, Kurt Franklin, and Carman helped start a revolution that changed what "Christian" music sounded like. Pioneers like these turned the negative view Christians had of cutting-edge music around.

Slowly many churches started to realize that music is a key element in reaching people, and that without using it to connect with the surrounding culture, a whole generation could be lost. There were certain artists and movements that played a key role in molding church worship into what it is today.

In an interview, I asked Dwayne Lacy, a journalist in a prominent *Gospel Magazine* and a dear friend, to give me some more insight on the people who had a part in the development of worship in the church during the past two decades. Here's what he said: "Hillsong Church had a huge part in influencing the way churches worship today. The whole idea of "corporate worship" caught on an album blew up and spread from there. Darlene Zschech was on the forefront of this movement, leading people close to God with her joyful spirit and sincere heart. Fred Hammond was another true trailblazer. He along with the West Angeles Church of God in Christ (Saints of Praise) helped to bring praise and worship as we know it into the predominantly African American churches with songs like "Inner Court" and "Spirit of David." Fred Hammond's music had a definite "urban edge" sound, which started to bleed over into churches of different denominations and color revolutionizing the worship scene of the '90s.

Of course I don't think anyone can talk about praise and worship without mentioning Ron Kenoly. His music truly transcended barriers and helped bring the church together. His sound of freedom and excellence spread around the world, changing the way people celebrated and even viewed God.

Then there was the British invasion. Delirious literally "rocked" the Christian music world as we knew it. Their sound, along with their cool accents, struck a common chord with people in and out of the church, drawing huge crowds into passionate relationships with Christ. With songs like "Majesty," "I Could Sing of Your Love Forever," and "History Maker," they brought people into the Christian music world buy the tens of thousands. This rock worship sound was so anointed and trendy that many other contemporary Christian artists started singing and writing worship songs that took over the radio waves." Today the majority of songs played on Christian radio are actually praise and worship songs because of artists like these.

This revolution in godly music has turned into a revival of souls and has brought masses of young people into God's Kingdom across the globe. Today artists and groups such as Planet Shakers, Hillsong United, Hillsong Young and Free, Bethel, Elevation Church, Lecrae, Israel Houghton, Tadashi, Toby Mac, KB, and Jesus Culture are on the cutting edge of the music industry, using their sounds to draw millions close to God. These anointed ministers have inspired many churches to change the genres of music in which they package their worship to reflect sounds that resonate with the people in their cities. I believe this was a necessary shift in the body of Christ, which has helped position us to have the greatest move of God the church has ever seen.

Now it is important to understand there are songs that have lyrics filled with hatred, hopelessness, and lusts that come out of this generation. I am, by no means, saying we should embrace those messages, but don't throw the baby out with the bathwater. Remember it's not the message that opens the heart, but the sound. We need to wholeheartedly accept these sounds and use them to fill our young people with words of life. Then this music can be used to open the door to our children's core so they can freely worship, which is our ultimate goal. When we label these new sounds ungodly, many young people who have dedicated their lives to God become like caged eagles. They can see the sky and know they were destined to soar but are not allowed out because the church is afraid they will fly away never to return. The Bible says in Ephesians 6:4 that we should not "provoke our children to wrath." This is talking about not putting unnecessary rules and regulations on the next generation. When we take our likes or preferences and turn them into standards of righteousness for others, we are tying weights on them they were never meant to carry. The sad part is, many not only slow down in the race of their destiny but give up altogether, never reaching the finish line.

Every generation has a sound. It is our job as mentors and leaders, not to crush this sound, but to harness it. Just like a windmill harnesses the wind to convert it into energy, we need to take the sounds of this generation and harness them to create an atmosphere of worship that changes their world and helps propel them into their destiny.

Chapter 10

The Handoff

You've heard the proverb, "The greatest accomplishment of a teacher is the success of a student." But I challenge that thought with this: If a teacher's greatest success is only the success of their student, then it all stops there. The greatest teachers are those not only interested in the success of a student, but in the "succession of a student," or should I say the successor of a student. If this baton of wisdom and love is passed on, then the teacher's impact on their world never stops.

Sometimes accomplishment and ambition blind people to the fact that their life is not forever. Instead of trying to find the quickest and most efficient way to do something, we should look for someone that we can impart into so that we can multiply ourselves. The mentality of "If you want something done right, you have to do it yourself" will eventually bottleneck your impact on this world. Our own success can be the very thing that keeps the next wave of accomplishment from being achieved. In order to ensure the rise of future champions, we must first pour into them and then make room for them. By this I mean get out of their way and let them do what they have been raised up to do. This does not mean leave them high and dry, but that we should step back, giving them room to make mistakes so they can learn how to recover from them. This will bring them strength to soar on their own so that when we are no longer there to help, they will be able to succeed without us and rise above life's challenges.

Earlier in this book, I talked about protecting and even sheltering the helpless and its importance in the eyes of God. There is a time for that, but when someone has enough inner strength and knowledge to run forward in their leg of the race, we must let them do so.

Let me give you an example. Say you are the anchor of a relay team. (This is the person who runs the last leg of the race and is usually the fastest.) The person before you draws close so you start moving forward, matching their stride. They are finally close enough to make the handoff and yell, "Stick!" Then as soon as they let go of the baton, they immediately grab your free hand and proceed to run alongside of you. If they don't let go, you will never reach your full stride. Yes, they were your predecessor, and yes, you needed them in every way to get started; but if they never let go, then you will never be freed to truly excel.

Just like that first runner needed to let go, we must recognize in life when it is time to let someone soar on their own. Sometimes this is extremely hard to do, especially when you have gone through hurtful or unfair times in life and don't want them to experience the same thing. If we let fear creep into our hearts, it can infect our love, turning it into worry for someone we care for. Make no mistake, worry and love are not the same thing. God said, "Perfect love cast out all fear" (1 John 4:18). When we love someone, it builds a strong urge to trust the greatness of God in them, believing for the best to come out. Of course there will be heavy opposition they must face, but just because we are not holding their hand does not mean they are alone. God, the Father, is always with them and everything we imparted into their life will stir them to run their course with integrity. This stirring is like a built-in compass that will guide them to give in to the right convictions.

Many times it takes a catastrophic event such as a death of a loved one, or something of that magnitude, to open our eyes to the importance of pouring into the next generation and handing them what we have. When things like this shake us, it gives us a glimpse of how short life really is. But we should not wait until life slaps us in the face with a wake-up call to be stirred to action because sometimes by then, it's too late. Every day our sons, daughters, grandchildren, neighborhood kids, young coworkers, and many others who look up to us are faced with challenges that require the strength we posses to overcome them. The sooner we pour into them a passion to fight and the courage to believe, the sooner they can start overcoming the challenges of life. We must stir ourselves to action because every second counts. You never know what someone may be going through. If we put off till tomorrow what we can do today to reach these youth, we may pass up someone's last chance. That girl who was in the corner not talking to anyone else may be getting ready to take her own life if no one shows that they care or that junior high boy who was disrupting the class may be getting ready to kill his parents because he hates what they have made him become. It may be that high school teen who is the new kid in the neighborhood who is contemplating joining a gang because he has no friends or family who will protect him. Maybe it's a seventh grade girl who is throwing herself at every boy that comes her way because she was sexually molested by her father, which made her feel worthless and unloved, or that teen that was arrested across the street for selling drugs may have felt that was the only thing he could ever excel at because his parents told him he would never amount to anything. These are actual stories that young people have told me about themselves. But the amazing thing was that all of them were touched just in time by a loving person who wasn't afraid to be a leader in their life.

In order to do so, we must press through our own insecurities and failures that hold us back, trusting God to give us the love that will change this generation. You may be imperfect. Who isn't? Stop waiting to overcome every flaw and become the perfect role model because it will never happen. There is only one position that requires perfection and that's our Savior's. Our job is just to posses selfless love and a pure heart as we strive to make a difference in the next generation.

Chapter 11

The Charge

God has given each one of us a sphere of influence. A segment of society that we see and touch on a regular basis in which he has called us to reach. Some may seem smaller than others, but they are all equally important. You may say, "I'm not someone who has the talent or fame to influence my world." Or you may be a prominent figure, with a huge platform such as a media personality, actor, pop star, pastor, or principal but think you have nothing to truly offer. It doesn't matter who you are, and it doesn't matter what your personality is, if you have fought the fight of life and are still standing strong, with faith and love, you posses something that this upcoming generation needs. Your story, strength, and passion are a lifeline to people coming up after you. No price can be placed on the value of someone taking the hand of a younger generation and showing them the way.

There was a man who lived many years ago who was known as a patriot. His heart burned with passion to see his people rise to their God-given place in this world. His dream was for his nation to find respect and freedom. Many challenges faced him as he strived to make a difference.

As an adopted orphan, he faced many insecurities and regrets that eventually turned to rage. In life, his general lack of communication skills coupled with a criminal history of violence made it extremely hard for him to gain an audience with anyone, much less change the course of history. Despite these setbacks, he could not ignore the purpose that had been branded in his heart. Because of his faith, love, and perseverance, he was able to help this people he cared so much for escape from the hell on earth they had been living in and move on to seek a new destiny.

Even though he had literally given the best years of his life for this purpose and was looked at as their leader, many of the very ones he helped turned on him. His own brother and sister started resenting him because of his accomplishments and stirred up others against him. But he never gave up. With his natural eyes, he saw people who had been freed, but deep down inside, he knew there was more. When he listened to what was inside of him, he knew not only was he supposed to help them find freedom, but that he needed to show them how to get to a place of spiritual prosperity, economic stability, and self-respect so their children's children could enjoy it as well. As he began to share this vision and lay out a plan of action, most of his peers thought he was crazy. Some even stirred up riots against him saying that he was naive and even senile to believe such outlandish things. They thought his beliefs would stir up false hope in young "feeble" minds, causing them to rise, only to be crushed by a cruel and powerful world around them. Because of this opposition, his dreams seemed to be shattered.

What this man hadn't realized was that all of his acts of love and words of encouragement had already infected the next generation. They had grown tired of hearing how their future was bleak at best from the leaders around them and were ready to hear a voice of confidence who dared to believe. This man's message, which he lived out, was so full of earnest expectation for their future that they could not help but be drawn to him. As he grew older, there was one young man in particular who was so touched by this man's purpose and personal humility that he wholeheartedly dedicated his life to serve alongside him. This young man followed the older man everywhere he went, taking in every word of passion and every act of wisdom. He became the man's right hand. He always was there to stand against the opposition with, and many times for, his beloved friend. Eventually, he started to believe in this dream just as much as his leader and would do anything to see it fulfilled.

Years later, this hope had spread throughout the entire young population. All of this man's naysayers and haters had passed on and a new generation of greatness had come to the forefront. The time had come for this people to rise up and be who they were created to be, but no one was as ready as the old man and his most committed disciple, who had become his spiritual son. Now the man was very old and knew he had left nothing undone. He had run his course and understood that his time was near, so he called for everyone to be assembled. With his son at his side, he gazed at the masses of young people who had grown to respect every word that came out of his mouth. He had become an icon in their world. A symbol of God's meekness and power all wrapped up in one. They waited to hear what words of instruction this legend of a man had for them. The moment he had dreamed of all his life was at hand. As he looked from side to side at the young people he so loved, he began to slowly realize that the final chapter in his own story was not his to write. In that moment, he began to fully grasp what was in his heart all along. That he was called to lead a generation out of hopelessness and entrapment, but he would send them, only seeing with his eyes as they went, into a place of greatness. No one knew more about this place than him. No one dreamed of this place more than him. No one deserved this place more than him. But in striving to bring a people to it his whole life, he had actually already found it for himself. In all reality, he had personally attained this place of prosperity, security, and opportunity even though he had never physically stepped foot in this land he knew was promised. As this realization sunk in, he turned and faced the young man he loved so much. This wasn't the same boy he saw so many years before running in fear and listening to the crowd. No, he had grown into a powerful man of God full of compassion and faith, ready to face all odds in order to see this God-given dream come to pass. Then he placed his hand on the side of the young man's check and said, "You lead them, my son." These words were the most bitter, yet sweetest words the young man had ever heard, cutting right to his heart. The man who started it all and believed against all odds was willing in a single moment to hand it all over. Then, with tears welling up in his eyes and a gentle smile of strength on his face, he said, "This is your destiny. Mine was to put it inside of you." He paused and looked into the young man's soul, seeing him transform into a champion of a leader before his very eyes. This single moment seemed like an eternity. Finally, the old man knowing his life's purpose was complete, embraced his disciple for the last time and departed. Then, full of strength, Joshua turned away and walked into his destiny. But he knew it was all possible only because a man named Moses first believed in him.

    This is one of the greatest stories of mentorship in history. It is a story of a man having a flame of love and compassion ignited in his heart and then spreading that flame. As Moses passed the torch of greatness to the next generation of his day, let us bring purpose and life, giving love to ours. No one can reach the young people God has placed in your sphere of influence like you can. There are masses of youth who are in desperate need of what you possess—your faith in God, your staying power, and your love. Never doubt the importance of what has been placed inside of you and always remember, you hold the key to unlock the full potential of the next generation.

ABOUT THE AUTHOR

Lane and Lisa Pastor Faith City Church in Cypress TX. They have been happily married for 17 years and they have three sons: Paul, Judah, and Levi. He holds a bachelor of science from Sam Houston State University and a bachelor of ministry from Indiana Christian University. Before starting Faith City Church he served on staff at Family Faith Church for more than twenty-two years as an associate pastor, youth pastor, and worship leader. He has built successful youth ministries of hundreds at Family Faith Church's three campuses and impacted thousands over twenty years. He is raising up three godly sons and has influenced many young people to become champions in life, while faithfully serving in many capacities in the local church. Lane's greatest desire is to follow Christ wholeheartedly while seeing his sons and this generation fulfill their destiny in Christ. His preaching inspires people to dream big and stretch beyond their limitations to accomplish more than they could ever imagine. His wife, Lisa, is a constant inspiration to him and shares his passion to see this next generation touch the world for Jesus Christ. When Lane leads worship, he ushers in God's presence and puts the focus on the heart of the Father. He does not do it to entertain but to build into this generation their intrinsic value and God's insatiable love he has for them. Lane and Lisa unashamedly love this generation of youth and stand for the greatness God has placed in them.

CPSIA information can be obtained
at www.ICGtesting.com
Printed in the USA
BVHW081735300919
559808BV00006B/816/P